Focus

The focus of this book is:

● to use the term 'sentence' correctly,
● to reinforce knowledge of sentences.

 **Tuning In**

The front cover

Let's read the title together.

Look at the photographs on the front cover.

What sort of information do you think will be in the book?

The back cover

Let's read the blurb together.

What does it tell us about the book?

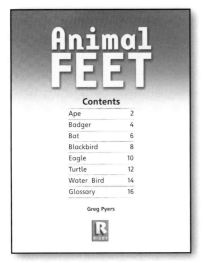

Contents

The contents page tells us what information is in the book, and helps us to find it. The entries are in page order, and in alphabetical order. Why do you think this might be?

Would someone like to suggest a section for us to find?

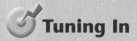

This is an ape.
It uses its feet to climb.

Prompt and Praise

Check the children are pausing at a full stop.

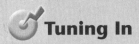 **Tuning In**

Where do apes live?

Who can find the words 'feet' and 'tree'?

It holds on to the tree with its feet.

 **Prompt and Praise**

Check the children are reading high frequency words fluently.

Praise children who are reading with expression.

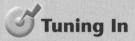

Tuning In

What animal is this?

What is it using its feet to do?

This is a badger.
It uses its feet to dig.

Prompt and Praise

Check the children are reading with good intonation, so that the sentences sound as if they make sense.

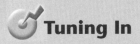 **Tuning In**

Where do badgers live?

Who can find the words 'digs', 'ground' and 'claws'?

It digs into the ground
with its **claws**.

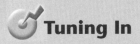 **Prompt and Praise**

Praise the children who read the text on page 5 as a complete
sentence.

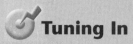

Tuning In

What animal is this?

What is unusual about it?

This is a bat.
It uses its feet to hang
upside down.

Prompt and Praise

Check the children are scanning the photographs for help with vocabulary.

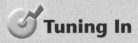

Tuning In

What does it use its feet to do?

Who can find the words 'hang', 'branch' and 'feet'?

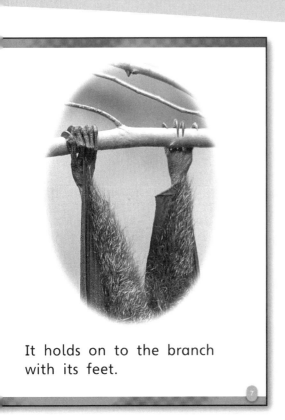

It holds on to the branch with its feet.

😃 Prompt and Praise

If the children are struggling with the new vocabulary, alert them to useful features of the words – consonant clusters like 'br', or the long 'ee' digraph.

Praise children who are reading with expression.

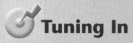 **Tuning In**

What bird is this?

Have you ever seen a blackbird?

What is it using its feet to do?

This is a blackbird.
It uses its feet to **perch**.

Prompt and Praise

Check the children pause at full stops.

Check the children can quickly move from the end of the first line to the start of the second on page 9.

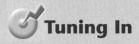

Tuning In

Why might a blackbird perch on a branch? (*to sing? to look for food? to rest? to look for enemies?*)

Who can find the words 'perch', 'feet' and 'branch'?

It holds on to the branch with its feet.

9

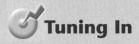

Prompt and Praise

Praise children who succeed in reading the new vocabulary in context. If they struggle, remind them to look carefully at the words, using initial letters or clusters and cross-checking with the pictures.

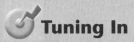

Tuning In

What bird is this?

What is it using its feet to do?

This is an eagle.
It uses its feet to catch fish.

Prompt and Praise

Check the children stop at full stops.

Tuning In

What do sea eagles eat?

Who can find 'catch', 'snatches', 'water', 'talons'?

It **snatches** fish from
the water with its **talons**.

Prompt and Praise

Praise children who tackle new vocabulary confidently.

If they are struggling, help them to decode the words by using
context and phoneme knowledge.

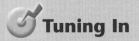
Tuning In

What animal is this?

What is it using its feet to do?

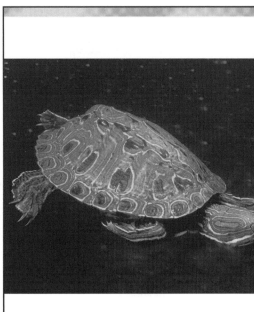

This is a turtle.
It uses its feet to swim.

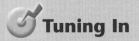
Prompt and Praise

Praise the children who read new vocabulary with confidence.

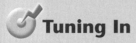 **Tuning In**

What is special about the turtle's feet?

Can you find the words 'webbed feet'?

It swims in the water
with its **webbed feet**.

 Prompt and Praise

Praise the children who read these two lines as one sentence.

13

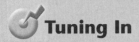 **Tuning In**

What is unusual about this water bird?

What is it using its feet to do?

This is a **water bird**.
It uses its feet to walk.

 **Prompt and Praise**

Check the children are dividing the sentences accurately.

Praise children who are reading with confidence.

Tuning In

Why are the plants called water lilies?

What might the bird be looking for?

It walks on the **water lilies** with its long toes.

Prompt and Praise

If a child is having difficulties with 'water lilies', prompt the use of the picture and initial letter clues.

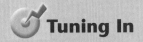 **Tuning In**

What do we use a glossary for?

What do you notice about the order of the words?

Why do you think 'water lilies' comes after 'water bird'?

Which two words almost mean the same? (*claws, talons*)

Glossary

claws	the hard, sharp nails on animals' feet
perch	to sit or stand on something for a short time
snatches	grabs something suddenly
talons	hooked claws
water bird	a type of bird that lives near water or marshland
water lilies	a type of plant with large, flat leaves that grows in water
webbed feet	feet that have a piece of skin that joins the toes

16

 Prompt and Praise

Check children realize that a word in **bold** signals an entry in the glossary.

Praise children who can remember where the word appeared in the text.